AF481705

# WHAT DO YOU KNOW ABOUT THE AMAZON?

## Nature for Kids
## Children's Nature Books

Speedy Publishing LLC

40 E. Main St. #1156

Newark, DE 19711

www.speedypublishing.com

Copyright 2017

All Rights reserved. No part of this book may be reproduced or used in any way or form or by any means whether electronic or mechanical, this means that you cannot record or photocopy any material ideas or tips that are provided in this book.

In this book, we're going to talk about the mighty Amazon River and its basin. So, let's get right to it!

The Amazon River in South America isn't just a river. It's actually a huge system of water. Its basin's rainforest is one of the largest ecosystems in the world. In terms of the volume of water it carries, as well as its width, it's considered to be the most massive river on planet Earth. The river provides a home for thousands of unique animals and plants.

Amazon River

Andes Mountains

# HOW LONG IS THE AMAZON RIVER?

The source of the Amazon River is in the Andes Mountains on the western coast of South America. The mountainous range acts as a barrier that prevents moist air from exiting on the west coast. Instead, there's intense rain in the region that feeds the Amazon's source on an almost consistent and continuous basis. From the mountains, it travels about 4,000 miles or about 6,437 kilometers winding its way through dense rainforests and wet lowlands until it reaches Brazil's northeastern coastline where it empties into the Atlantic Ocean.

There's still some debate whether the Nile River or the Amazon River is the longest since rivers are extremely difficult to measure. It's believed that the Nile River is a little longer at 4,258 miles or about 6,873 kilometers. One thing that is known for certain is that the Amazon carries a larger volume of water than any other river on Earth.

Amazon Rainforest

Its system of drainage is the largest such river system in the world. It's estimated that the river carries about 20% of Earth's freshwater. It drains more water out than the water drained out by the next largest six rivers in total. Its basin is a maze of tributaries. There are over 1,000 tributaries and 17 of these are over 900 miles long.

# WHAT IS THE WIDTH OF THE AMAZON RIVER?

Even the Amazon River has periods when it doesn't have as much volume as it has at other times. Its dry season is from the months of June through November. During that time, it averages about 2 to as much as 6 miles in width. However, in the flood season from December to April, its width can swell to 30 miles across! When the waters are flowing fast, the current goes at a clip of 4 miles per hour. The river is so wide that bridges can't be built to cross it.

Francisco de Orellana

# HOW DID THE AMAZON RIVER GET ITS NAME?

Around 1541 AD a soldier from Spain, called Francisco de Orellana, began to explore the Amazon. It's believed that he was the first European man to do so. During his travels, he encountered some huge women warriors. He named them the Amazons after the women warriors in Greek myths. That's how the river was named.

# HOW BIG IS THE AMAZON BASIN?

The Amazon basin is so large that it is situated in parts of six different countries including Brazil, Bolivia, Ecuador, Venezuela, Columbia, and Peru. Over 66% of the basin is completely covered with selva, which is the rainforest. The basin is approximately 38% of South America's total landmass and is about 2.7 million square miles or 7 million square kilometers.

Amazon River

Amazon River basin

The lowlands that surround the river and its many tributaries flood every year and they enrich the soil. The rainforest's interior has many types of plants and animals. Just one hectare of forest area, which is about 2.5 acres, has as many as 250 different species of densely packed trees.

Despite the difficulties of getting from place to place in the river basin area, there are several large cities located there. Belem in Brazil, which is located at the mouth of the river and is home to over 1.3 million people.

Santarem in Brazil, which is located where the Amazon River crosses the Tapajos River.

Manaus in Brazil, which is located in the center of the jungle area and has a population of 2 million.

Iquitos in Peru, which is a port as well as a gateway to the native villages of the northern Amazon area.

Of the people who live in the Amazon basin area, about 9 percent are descended from native peoples. There are over 300 different native groups and more than 60 groups are living in very isolated areas.

Aerial View of Amazon River

# WHICH ANIMALS LIVE IN THE AMAZON RIVER?

Over 5,000 fish species live in the Amazon River. Electric fish, over 100 different species of them, swim in the river as do 60 different species of piranhas. Piranhas are feared but they rarely attack humans. They are dangerous though. They have been known to eat small mammals and they can smell a few drops of blood in 200 liters of water. The arapaima, also known as the pirarucu, fish lives in the Amazon. One of the largest of all types of freshwater fish on Earth, it regularly reaches a length of 15 feet. There are several other interesting water creatures too including:

The Amazon River dolphin, which is the largest of all river dolphins worldwide and changes from a gray color to a pink color to white over the course of its life.

The giant otter, a carnivorous mammal is the longest member of the weasel family.

The Amazonian manatee, a slow, large, strange-looking creature.

# WHAT IS THE RIVER REEF?

When the Amazon River empties into the ocean it creates what is known as the Amazon plume. It's the area where the freshwater fans out into the Atlantic Ocean. The water pours out with tremendous force.

It stretches out as far as the Caribbean Sea. Because it is freshwater flowing into salt water, it affects the percentage of salt in the water it flows into. It also affects the temperature of the water and the amount of sediment in the water. The churning plume of water goes down about 65 feet from the water's surface.

Recently an international group of scientists discovered something amazing under this plume. They found coral reefs living underneath where the plume was flowing out. They were very surprised because it meant that corals were growing in a very dark environment with almost no penetration of sunlight.

The underwater creatures that live there are also surviving in a very fast-paced current so it's not clear how they are getting their food. More scientific expeditions will be needed to determine more about these unique reefs.

Amazon Jungle

# WHICH ANIMALS AND PLANTS LIVE IN THE RAINFOREST?

Scientists believe that the Amazon rainforest can be considered "Earth's lungs." The millions of plants that live there absorb vast amounts of carbon dioxide and as a by-product they release the life-giving oxygen that humans and animals need to live. Without the Amazon rainforest, it's doubtful that life on Earth would survive. Conservationists have been working to protect this vital ecosystem.

The rainforest of the Amazon River is home to over one-third of all the species known worldwide. The area has incredible biodiversity. There are sometimes as many as 100 different tree species on a single acre of land. Some of the interesting animals in the rainforest include:

The spider monkey, which lives in the forest canopy.

The golden lion tamarin, which is also a type of monkey that has an orange lion-like mane.

The sloth, which barely moves
and rarely climbs down.

The giant anteater, which hunts ants
and termites on the forest floor.

The capybara, which is the largest rodent on Earth.

The toucan, which is a
bird with a colorful beak.

The scarlet macaw, which is a type of parrot.

The black caiman, which is the Amazon River's largest predator and similar to a crocodile.

The anaconda, which is an enormous snake that has been known to kill humans and that squeezes its victims to death.

The jaguar, which is a huge wild cat and one of the most dangerous animals in the rainforest.

# WHAT ARE THE NAMES OF THE FOREST LAYERS?

The Amazon rainforest has four distinct layers: The emergent layer, which has giant trees that grow over 200 feet tall and pop out above the canopy

The canopy, which consists of the crowns of trees and houses a large portion of the animal species

The understory, which is very dark and doesn't receive much sunlight

The forest floor, which has decaying plants

# ARE THERE PIRATES ON THE AMAZON RIVER?

Because there are very few roadways and the jungle is next to impossible to navigate, the Amazon River is vital to the transportation system in South America. Many native people depend solely on the river to get back and forth. Ships of all sizes move tourists as well as supplies from one area of the basin to another.

The waterways aren't supervised or policed so there has been a rise in crime and hijackings by pirates that want to steal whatever is on board. Hollywood movies have made pirates into likeable characters, but true pirates are scary criminals that terrorize visitors as well as the native people.

# SUMMARY

The Amazon River is so large that it carries 20% of the Earth's freshwater. The river is so powerful and so wide that bridges can't be built to cross it. The Amazon basin covers 38% of South America's landmass and is home to huge numbers of different animals and plants as well as native peoples.

Awesome! Now that you know about the Amazon River and its basin, you can read more interesting information about Earth's major rivers in Baby Professor books like The Longest Rivers Lead to the Biggest Oceans.

Visit
BABY PROFESSOR
EDUCATION KIDS
www.BabyProfessorBooks.com
to download Free Baby Professor eBooks
and view our catalog of new and exciting
Children's Books

www.ingramcontent.com/pod-product-compliance
Lightning Source LLC
Chambersburg PA
CBHW060615120726
48002CB00010B/2983